SPORTS CLASSIC
HIGHLIGHTS
Recipes

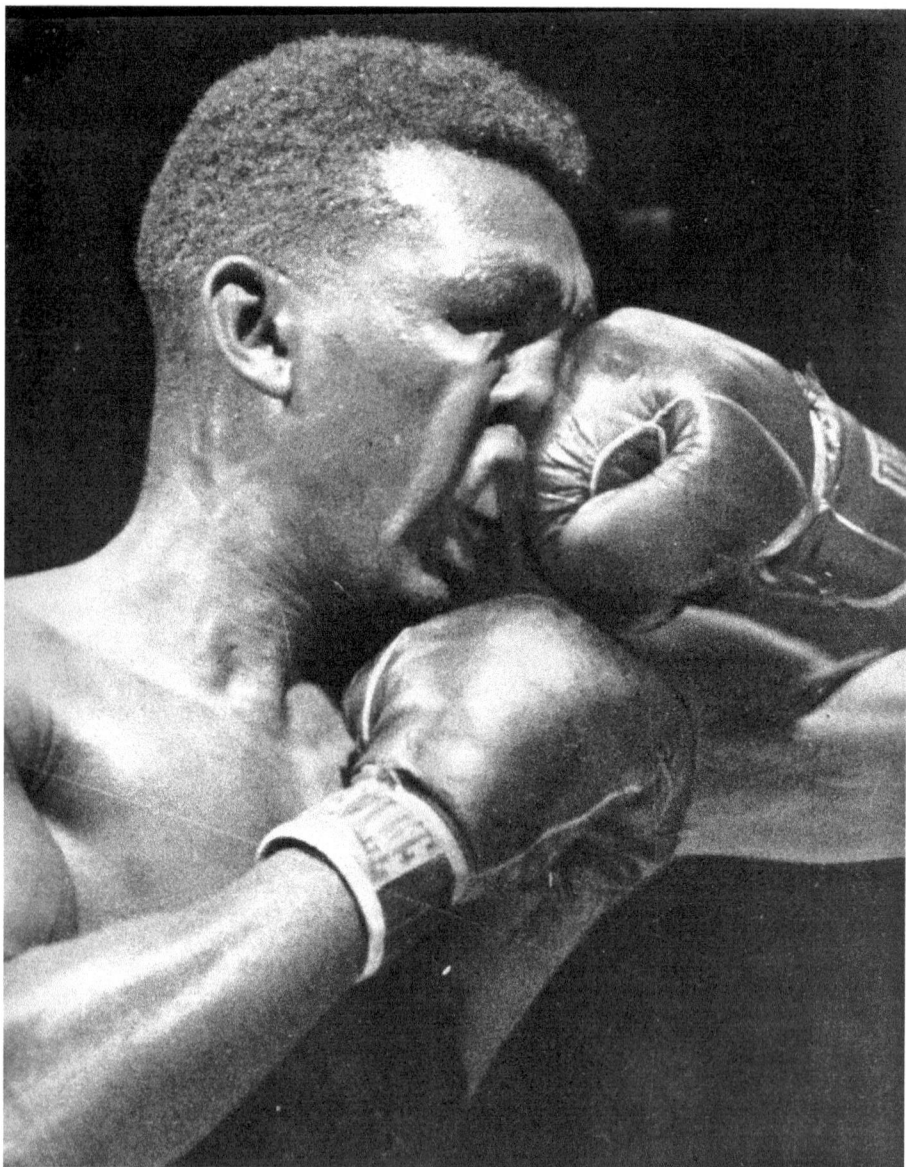

Many thanks, to Melodee for the photo images.

Lone Moon publications

Introduction:

Fresh blended drinks and tasty treats for a party or during a game with friends. . .

I've sampled many different types of snack foods, drinks and appetizers at parties and homes of friends.
In my travels, I've prepared many different foods, dips and drink concoctions for others.
Many, can be prepared in 15 minutes or less.
Some of these, I will share with you here.

So, peel off all layers of egotism and self pity.
Cut all thoughts of unkindness and unhappy moments from your mind.
Remove all prejudices and worries.
Remember life is worth living, no matter how the ball bounces.
Optimism and love with strong determination and living at your highest, every moment that you can, will allow you to achieve your greatest accomplishments in life.
Smiles and pleasant words to friends and others, courageousness yet gentleness enhances growth in life.
Now, lets enjoy.

Tbsp = Tablespoon

Tsp = Teaspoon

Qt   = Quart

Add salt according to health and taste in the recipes that call for salt.

JUICE DRINKS

Spicy Cranberry Juice Drink

3 cups cranberries

2 slices lemon

4 whole cloves

1 teaspoon cinnamon

1 cup sugar (use sugar to taste)

2 Qt. water

Place cranberries, lemon, spices and water in covered saucepan. Cook until steaming on low heat until cranberries are tender. Strain, dissolve sugar in the hot juice. Chill, serve cold.

Apple Pineapple Juice Drink

3 cups apple juice
1 cup pineapple juice
1/3 cup diced pineapples
Pinch of salt
½ cup of crushed ice
8 strawberries, diced
1/3 cup sugar (optional)

Place apple juice, pineapple juice, diced pineapples, diced strawberries, crushed ice and sugar in a tall pitcher stir well and serve.

Fruity Banana Punch Drink

4 bananas   1 cup sugar
6 cups water   2 (32 oz.) can
of pineapple/grapefruit juice
1 (8 oz.) can frozen orange juice
  concentrate

Blend bananas and water in blender. Then mix with the rest of ingredients (with the exception of the frozen orange juice concentrate) in large container. Refrigerate.
To serve: pour 1 quart of 7-Up or ginger ale in a pitcher or large bowl add contents of the punch from the large container then add the 8 oz. can frozen orange juice. Stir then Serve.

Carrot Pineapple Juice Drink

32 oz. pineapple juice
2 medium carrots (small pieces)
2 slices of lemon
1 cup crushed ice
1/3 cup sugar (optional)

Place pineapple juice, lemon and carrots into blender. Bump blender until carrots are liquefied. Serve in two tall glasses over crushed Ice.

Knock Out Fruit Punch Drink

1 cup real lemon juice

2 (32 oz.) cans orange juice

1 (32 oz.) can apricot nectar

2 pkg. raspberry koolaide

1 can pineapple juice

1` small can chopped pineapple

1-2 cup sugar

Mix all ingredients together and place in a large container. Freeze. Remove from freezer 5 hours before serving to allow it to start to get slushy. Just before serving add ginger ale or 7 up to desired taste and texture.

Grape Lemonade Juice Drink

Squeeze juice from 3 lemons
½ cup sugar
1 - 32 oz grape juice
1 - 16 oz water
1 - quart container of ice cubes

Combine lemon juice, sugar and water, stir then add grape juice and stir again. Chill, then Fill 8 oz glass with ice cubes. Place a slice of lemon on each glass. Pour & serve.

Orange So Good

1 - 8 oz can frozen orange juice
1 - 12 oz water   1 egg
1 - 12 oz can milk   1- 2 cup sugar
1 cup cracked ice
1 cup vanilla ice cream

  Add all ingredients at once to blender jar. Blend on high-speed for 1 minute.   Serve

Hotty Totty Tomato Drink

2 (12 oz cans beef broth)
2 (32 oz cans tomato juice)
¼ cup sherry or bourbon
2 lemon slices
6 whole cloves
1/8 tsp basil
1/8 tsp salt
½ tsp sugar
¼ tsp accent

Combine all ingredients in a pot and simmer for 5 minutes. Serve hot in mugs. This should warm you up.

Easy Time Punch

4 (12 oz.) cans pineapple juice concentrate
2 (12 oz.) cans limeade concentrate
1 (64 oz.) bottle lemon/lime soda
8 lemon slices

Combine the juice concentrates and fresh lemon slices the night before in a closed container, refrigerate overnight. The next day place in a large pitcher or punch bowl. Add the carbonated soda just before serving.

Young Folks Cold Sip

1 qt. lime sherbet
1 qt. ginger ale
1 qt. orange soda

Mix ½ quart ginger ale with lime sherbet. Allow sherbet to melt to a soupy mixture, then add orange soda. Just before serving add other ½ quart ginger ale but do not mix.

Warm up Nectar

3 cups water
¾ cup sugar
10 whole cloves
2 sticks cinnamon

Boil cinnamon sticks, cloves and water together in a pot for 5 minutes. Strain in a pitcher or large container, then add:

1 qt. apricot nectar
¼ cup lemon juice
1 cup strained freshly made strong tea.
Cool. Reheat before serving.
Good for when it's cold outside.

Hot Cider

1 qt. apple cider or apple juice
1 pt. cranberry juice
1 pt. orange juice
½ cup sugar
1 tsp. whole allspice
1 tsp. whole cloves
3 cinnamon sticks

Combine apple cider, cranberry juice and spices in a pot. Simmer for 5 - 10 minutes. Strain then put back in the pot while still hot. Add the sugar and orange juice, reheat. Stir then serve hot.
A great hot tangy drink when it's cold outside.

Chill Out Slush

1 qt. raspberry sherbet
1 (16 oz.) can frozen pink
lemonade
1 (32 oz) Ginger ale or
Champagne

Mix sherbet and lemonade
concentrate together. Just before
serving, slowly add ginger ale or
Champagne for the most delicious
and refreshing drink. Oh, yea.

GEORGE SILK / *Do-or-die catch* '43

MARVIN E. NEWMAN / *Olympic swimmer* 51

COFFEE DRINKS & PUNCH

Iced coffee

Prepare a pot of strong blend drip coffee. Pour 12 oz. cooled into a pitcher with 6 oz. of chilled milk. Add 3 tablespoon of chocolate syrup and sugar to taste. Pour over crushed Ice in a tall glass. Top with whipped cream and shaved chocolate.

On The Run Mocha Mix

½ cup dry non dairy creamer
½ cup cocoa mix
½ cup sugar
½ tsp cinnamon
½ tsp nutmeg

Blend all ingredients together in a airtight container with lid. Shake well to blend well. Mix 1 - 2 tablespoon in a cup of strong brewed coffee (mix in, according to taste). Keep the rest stored for the next cup of coffee.

Creamy Coffee Soda

1 cup strong blend brewed
coffee, cooled
2 tablespoons sugar
¾ cup ice cream
½ cup ginger ale, chilled

Mix ½ of the coffee and sugar in a tall glass and stir. Add ½ of the ice cream, stir in ½ of the soda and serve at once. Top with maraschino cherry. Makes two tall cups.

Almond Coffee Float

1 cup strong brewed coffee (cooled)
1 cup milk
2 tablespoons brown sugar
dash salt
¼ teaspoon almond extract
1 cup chocolate or vanilla ice cream

Stir together milk, sugar, salt and extract. Stir well and pour in two tall glasses half filled with coffee. Top each with a scoop of ice cream.

Hot warm me up Brew

2 tablespoon hot milk

1 cup strong brewed coffee

2 tablespoons brown sugar

1/8 teaspoon cinnamon

1 shot brandy or cognac

Combine all ingredients in large mug, stir well. Serve hot with additional cinnamon on top

Creamy Coffee Punch

4 cups strong brewed coffee (cooled)
1/3 cup sugar (sweeten to taste)
½ cups milk
2 teaspoons vanilla extract
½ cup light cream or half-and-half
2 eggs well beaten
1 quart vanilla ice cream, softened

Stir into large pitcher or container: coffee, cold milk, sugar and vanilla extract. Stir cream into two well beaten eggs. Add to coffee mixture then blend in softened ice cream. Chill at least one hour before serving. Stir to blend then pour.

Creamy Coffee Pudding

1 package Jell-o vanilla
flavored pudding
1 ½ cup strong brewed coffee
½ cup milk
1 cup Cool Whip non-dairy
whipped topping

Combine pudding mix, coffee and milk in saucepan. Simmer and stir over low heat until mixture comes together. Stop and pour into a bowl. Place foil directly on surface of the bowl, chill thoroughly. Afterward beat until smooth. Fold in whipped topping. Serve in individual small bowls or glasses. Top with strawberries and whipped cream.

DAIRY DRINKS

Hot Chocolate

¼ cup unsweetened powdered cocoa
1/8 cup sugar (sweeten to taste)
¼ teaspoon vanilla extract
2 cups hot milk
¼ teaspoon salt

Blend all ingredients together. Serve hot in two tall mugs, topped with a dash of cinnamon, whipped cream and a marshmallow.

Peach Cooler

1 cup cold milk

1 cup chilled peaches, fresh or canned

1/4 teaspoon salt

1 or 2 drops almond extract

2 drops vanilla extract

1 cup vanilla ice cream

Place all ingredients except ice cream into a blender container, cover and process until smooth. Stop add ice cream, and process at high speed. Pour into tall glass and serve

Egg Nog

1 egg   1 cup milk
4 - 5 tbsp sugar   1 shot rum
dash nutmeg   dash salt

Beat egg yolk, add sugar, salt and milk. Then add stiffly beaten egg white, rum and nutmeg. Top with whipped cream.

Chocolate Vanilla Milkshake

¾ cup milk
½ cup vanilla ice cream
½ cup chocolate ice cream
½ tsp vanilla extract
½ tsp cocoa
1 - tbsp sugar

Place all ingredients into blender. Bump around in blender. Pour into a tall glass and top with a scoop caramel ice cream

Butterscotch Milkshake

1 - cup milk

¼ - teaspoon nutmeg

½ - cup vanilla ice cream

2 - teaspoon butterscotch sauce

½ - teaspoon vanilla extract

Place all ingredients together in blender. Bump around in blender. Pour into a tall glass top with a scoop of vanilla ice cream or whipped cream.

Pineapple Milk shake

½ cup milk
¼ cup pineapple sherbet
¼ cup diced or chopped pineapple
½ cup vanilla ice cream

Place all ingredients into blender. Bump around in blender. Pour into a tall glass. Top with whipped cream.

To make a milk shake thicker just add more ice cream in blender bump slowly in short bursts. Watch for desired thickness.

Orange Milkshake

¼ cup frozen orange juice concentrate

½ cup milk (or 1/3 cup carbonated orange soda)

¼ cup orange sherbet

½ cup vanilla ice cream

 2 tbsp sugar

Pour orange juice concentrate into blender. Add sugar, orange sherbet vanilla ice cream and milk (or carbonated orange soda). Bump around in blender. Pour into tall chilled glass then float on top a scoop of vanilla ice cream. Garnish with a slice of orange.

Banana Frosted milk shake

1 - banana   4 - tbsp sugar
½ cup cold milk
¼ tbsp vanilla extract
1 - cup vanilla ice cream
Add dash of nutmeg

Bump all ingredients around in a blender. Stop, Serve in tall glass (to make sweeter add a little more sugar in blender)

SANDWICHES

Olive Walnut Sandwich

½ cup chopped olives
½ cup chopped walnuts
3 tablespoons French dressing

Mix olives, walnuts and salad dressing. Spread on lightly buttered slices of wheat bread.

Ham Pistachio Sandwich

1 cup finely chopped ham
½ cup chopped pistachios
1 teaspoon spicy brown mustard

4 tablespoons mayonnaise or
salad dressing
pinch of black or white pepper
½ teaspoon lemon juice

Mix all ingredients together.
Butter slices of whole wheat toast
then spread ham nut mixture.

Date Pecan Sandwich

2 tablespoons orange juice
1 tablespoon orange rind
2 tablespoons French dressing
1 cup chopped dates
½ cup chopped pecans

Add orange juice, rind and French

dressing to dates and pecans. Mix well. Spread on lightly buttered slices of wheat toast with lettuce.

El Rancho Tall Boy Sandwich

Slice open a cheese / jalapeno hard roll (or plain hard roll)
1 slices of Bologna fried
2 slices of onion fried
2 slices of tomato
2 slices of hard salami
2 lettuce leaves
1 slice of Smoked Ham fried
4 thin cucumber slices
1 tbsp mayonnaise
1 tbsp mustard

Place all between hard roll and eat.

Cowboy Sauerkraut Little Smoky Sandwich

In a large frying pan, heat a small can of sauerkraut. Add in 10 Little Smoky beef or pork sausage. Cut into small cubes. Place mayonnaise, tomato and lettuce on one side of dark rye bread or hard roll and mustard on other side (add melted cheese of your choice optional). Cut into 4 parts and serve.

Steak Onion Bell Pepper Sandwich

2 ½ tablespoon olive oil

1 red onion sliced

1 lb. pound sirloin steak, cut
into thin strips

¼ teaspoon ground cumin

¼ teaspoon dried ground thyme

3 oz. sliced back olives

4 pita bread round halves

1 tablespoon onion powder

1 teaspoon black or white
pepper

1 teaspoon salt

1 teaspoon curry

1 sliced tomato

2 tablespoons mayonnaise or
salad dressing

¼ small cabbage shredded

Heat 2 tablespoons oil in heavy
medium non stick skillet over
medium low heat. Add the bell

pepper, onion and onion powder. Season with salt and pepper, cook until onion and bell pepper are very tender and beginning to brown. Stirring occasionally, add steak and place cover over skillet. Cook for 3-5 minutes. Stir and flip meat, bell pepper and onion. Keeping a watchful eye on your pot. Cook until meat is browned. Add cumin, thyme and curry. Stir one or two more minutes.

Remove from heat and mix in black olives. Spread mayonnaise onto pita breads then spoon the hot steak mix in. Top with the tomato slices and shredded cabbage.

Toasted Mozzarella Cheese Sandwich

10 ounces ricotta cheese
4 ounces mozzarella cheese shredded
½ cup thinly sliced salami
1 chopped tomato
1 small egg beaten to blend
little salt-and-pepper
10 slices of rye or wheat bread
3 tablespoons butter
3 tablespoons olive oil

Combine all ingredients together except the butter and olive oil. Blend in a bowl and spread on 5 slices of bread. Melt butter with oil in heavy large nonstick skillet over medium heat. Place the five slices of bread with the cheese spread, in the heated skillet then top with the remaining slices of bread. Cook until bread is toasted, then flip over cook other side until bread is toasted and cheese is melted (around 2 - 4 minutes). Serve hot.

DIPS

Ham dip

½ lb boiled, pressed or smoked
ham.
cream cheese or mayonnaise

Place meat in blender or food
processor until minced. Place in
bowl and mix with cream cheese or
mayonnaise. Place on platter and
garnish platter with assorted
crackers and chips or ¼ slices of
wheat or rye toast.

Beef Tongue Dip

½ lb beef tongue
spicy mustard

37

horseradish

1 - tbsp onion salt

1 - tsp black pepper

Boil or bake beef.
Add onion powder and black pepper
to tongue while cooking. Cook until
tender. Slice in thin slices. Serve on
platter. Place mustard and
horseradish in center of platter.
Surround with assorted crackers
and or toasted bread squares.

Chicken Liver Dip

Cook ½ lb chicken liver until
tender. Place in food processor or

blender, mix to a paste by adding melted butter and season with salt and pepper and onion powder.

Serve on a platter with crackers chips or toast.

Avocado Dip

1 ½ cup mashed avocado
1 teaspoon onion powder
1 teaspoon pepper
½ teaspoon cayenne
2 tablespoons lemon juice
2 tablespoons chili sauce (optional)

Cut avocado in half, remove seed and peel. Mash avocado in blender. Add other ingredients and blend. Serve with crackers or toast. Keep stored in a container in the refrigerator until time to serve.

Desert Dip

2 teaspoons cocoa
½ cup cold milk
½ teaspoon vanilla
8 oz whipped cream

Blend cocoa, milk and vanilla. Use blender or electric mixer, add whipped cream to the mix and whip

until light and fluffy. Serve in a
bowl on a platter with cookies and
pound cake strips.

Dipping Sauce

Sauces are associated with all
types of dips. These sauce recipes
can be easily blended and used to
dip hard roll pieces, soft roll pieces,
sandwiches, toast, crackers, chips,
cut bread squares, rolled beef,
diced pork, egg rolls, shrimp,
cheese and any other food that you
can stick a tooth pick thru and dip.
Place a few different type sauce dip
in small cups on a platter, garnish
and let

41

your guest decide what sauce they like the best.

Hollandaise Dipping Sauce

1 medium onion, finely chopped
6 parsley sprigs, chopped
½ teaspoon tarragon
2 tablespoons tarragon vinegar
¾ cup hollandaise sauce
¼ teaspoon onion powder

Place onion, parsley, tarragon and vinegar in small saucepan. Heat to boiling and cook until liquid is evaporated. Mix well with Hollandaise sauce and onion powder. Serve warm.

Dill Dipping Sauce

1 cup sour cream
2 medium dill pickles, chopped
1 ½ teaspoons dill weed
Dash of salt and pepper

Combine ingredients. Mix well. Keep refrigerated in air tight container until time to serve.

Horseradish Dipping Sauce

One slice dried bread, finely crumbled
½ cup prepared horseradish
½ cup light cream
1 tablespoon sugar
¼ teaspoon salt

Dash of Pepper

½ cup heavy cream

Combine ingredients except cream. Whip cream and fold into horseradish mixture. Keep refrigerated in air tight container until time to serve.

Spicy Curried Walnut & Coconut Dipping Sauce

½ cup salted walnuts, finely chopped

½ cup finely grated coconut

1 teaspoon curry powder

1 tablespoon milk

½ teaspoon Tabasco sauce

Combine ingredients with mayonnaise to your taste mix well and serve.

Caper Mayonnaise Dip

½ cup mayonnaise
¼ cup capers, drained
¼ cup lemon juice
½ teaspoon onion salt
¼ teaspoon Tabasco sauce

Combine ingredients. Mix well. Keep refrigerated in a air tight container until time to serve.

Tarter Sauce Dip

½ cup mayonnaise
10 green olives
2 teaspoons onion powder
3 chopped, sweet pickles
2 tablespoons capers

Combine ingredients. Mix well.
Keep refrigerated in an air tight
container until serving time.

Hot Mustard Dipping Sauce

½ cup dry mustard
¼ cup hot water
1 tablespoon olive oil
1 teaspoon salt
1 juicy chili pepper (optional)

Combine dry mustard and hot water. Add water slowly because you want the mix to be creamy not watery. Then add salt, olive oil (and diced chili pepper with its juices optional). Mix well. Allow to stand at room temperature for 15 to 20 minutes to develop flavor than serve.

Sweet & Sour Dipping Sauce

1 pint peach preserves
2 oz pimientos, drained and
Chopped finely
¼ cup white vinegar

Combine ingredients. Mix well.

Keep refrigerated in air tight container until time to serve.

Teriyaki Sauce

4 tablespoons cornstarch
1/3 cup soy sauce
¼ cup sugar
1 clove Garlic, minced
2 tablespoon minced fresh ginger
¼ cup dry white wine
1 cups beef broth

Blend all ingredients together in a saucepan, except wine. Heat, then add wine. Stirring until light creamy.

Meatballs
(go great with most sauces)

2 pounds ground beef
(or 1 lb. beef and 1 lb. pork)
½ cup fine dry bread crumbs
½ cup milk
½ cup minced onion
1 tablespoon onion powder
2 teaspoon salt
½ teaspoon curry
2 teaspoon pepper

Combine ingredients in bowl, mixing lightly to blend. Shape into small balls. Fry in oil in a skillet at medium heat until browned or (bake in the oven until brown, arrange on shallow baking pan bake in oven at 500° for 4 to 5 minutes until lightly browned, remove from oven. Stick a toothpick through each one and place on a platter with dipping sauce in the center of the platter.

Cheese Balls
(go great with some sauces)

1 (16 oz.) cream cheese
1 (3 oz) blue cheese
1 teaspoon Tabasco sauce
1 teaspoon Worcestershire sauce
1 minced garlic clove
½ cup chopped finely toasted
 Almonds

Softened cheese. Mix ingredients into cheese except almonds. Shape into small balls. Chill 4 hrs. in refrigerator. Remove, roll in almonds. Serve with crackers on a platter, place dip in center of platter.

Superb Soy Sauce Dip

3 tablespoon butter
1 cup water
5 tablespoon soy sauce paste
3 tablespoon cornstarch
¼ teaspoon onion powder

Melt butter in skillet. Add water and heat to boiling. Add concentrated soy sauce or soy paste and cornstarch. Cook and stir until thickened. Serve warm

Orange Honey Dipping Sauce

½ cup butter
1 cup heavy cream
¼ cup orange marmalade
2 ½ tablespoon cornstarch
¼ cup orange liqueur
¼ cup honey

Heat butter and cream in skillet continue stirring then add honey and marmalade. As ingredients begin to melt mix in cornstarch and orange liqueur, continue to stir until thickened. Serve warm.

COCKTAIL SAUCE

6 tablespoons ketchup
3 tablespoons lemon juice
1 tablespoon grated horseradish
6 drops Tabasco sauce
1 teaspoon Worcestershire sauce
dash celery salt (or salt)
dash onion powder

Combine all ingredients, adding salt and celery salt to taste. Chill before serving with shellfish.

COTTAGE CHEESE

Cottage cheese is a concentrated form of milk. 1 pound of cottage cheese contains most of the protein, calcium, phosphorus, iron and vitamins found in 3 quarts of milk.

3 ounces of cottage cheese furnishes about 50% of an adults daily requirement for calcium. Cottage cheese is a complete protein (builds, repairs, and maintains body tissue).

It is desirable for growing children and is a great food for adults. Cottage cheese is easily digested. It has a high nutritional value and low-calorie content. 1 ounce of creamed cottage cheese is about 30 calories. It combines nicely with almost any type of food.

COTTAGE CHEESE FRUIT DRESSING

½ cup cottage cheese
½ cup cream
1 bowl of fruit mixed some
 diced
½ cup lemon juice
½ teaspoon salt
2 tablespoon honey or sugar
1 tablespoon chopped chives

Blend and beat all Ingredients together until smooth. Pour over fruit bowl.

COTTAGE CHEESE ROLLS

1 cup cottage cheese

½ teaspoon Worcestershire
sauce
2 tablespoons chili sauce
little salt and pepper
thin slices of thin sliced beef

Mix cheese, sauces and
seasonings. spread onto the beef,
roll and fasten with tooth picks.
(could also wrap a leaf of spinach
around the beef) then faster with
toothpicks. Good for dipping in
sauce.

CHEESE SPREAD

2 cups sieved cottage cheese
few drops of onion juice
1 tablespoon bouillon paste

Drain excess moisture from cottage cheese and force through a sieve or whip until smooth. Combined with bouillon paste and onion juice. Beat to blend. Chill until ready to use. Use as a spread on crisp wafers or as a dip.

COTTAGE & CREAM CHEESE SPREAD

1 cup cottage cheese
¼ cup sour cream
little salt and pepper

Mix cottage cheese and sour cream together. Blend until smooth. (optional other seasonings you could use: poppy seeds, garlic, onion powder or herbs). Serve as a spread or dip for chips.

Vegetable Cheese Dip

 8 ounces cream cheese
1 tablespoon finely grated carrot
1 tablespoon finely chopped Parsley
2 teaspoons onion powder
¼ teaspoon salt
½ teaspoon Worcestershire Sauce.

Combined all ingredients blend well and chill. Serve in a bowl on a platter of raw vegetables.

AVOCATO SPREAD

1 cup smooth blended cottage
 cheese
 little salt and pepper
 horseradish
onion powder
Mayonnaise or cream
1 mashed avocado

Mix cottage cheese with avocado
and seasoning.Thin with cream or
mayonnaise. Serve as a dip for
potato or other type chips

STUFFED CELERY

Fill crisp stalks of celery with

cottage cheese or cream cheese.
Arrange them on a round plate, fill
the center with olives. Serve

FILLED TOMATOES

6 medium tomatoes
2 cups whipped cheese
¼ cup salad dressing or
mayonnaise
1 tablespoon chopped pickle
1 tablespoon minced onion
3 tablespoons chopped
pimiento
3 tablespoons chopped walnut
optional ½ cup chop beef or pork

Cut the top off the tomatoes

and scoop out center. Sprinkle with salt, combine remaining ingredients and mix well. Then filled the tomato cups. Chill thoroughly. Serve on lettuce with additional mayonnaise.

CHEESE FRUIT CHILL

1 package flavored gelatin
1 cup hot water
½ cup creamy cottage cheese
1 cup heavy cream, whipped
½ cup walnut halves, broken
½ cup maraschino cherries quartered
1 cup crushed pineapple, well drained.
Dissolve gelatin in hot water.

Chill until partially set. Fold in cottage cheese, whipped cream, walnuts, cherries and pineapple. Pour into 1 quart refrigerator tray. Chill until firm. Cut and serve.

PEACH PARTY DOWN LOAF

2 packages lemon flavored gelatin
¼ teaspoon salt
1 cup peach syrup
1 ½ cup grapefruit juice
1 ½ cup drained sliced cling peaches
2 tablespoons chopped pimiento
1 ¼ cups cottage cheese
½ cup chopped celery

2 tablespoons chopped parsley
½ teaspoon onion powder

Warm peach syrup and grapefruit juice. Dissolve gelatin add salt. Cool until slightly thickened. Arrange peaches and pimiento in bottom of an oiled loaf pan 8"x6"x4" cover with half the gelatin mixture. Chill until firm. Add cottage cheese, celery, parsley and onion powder. Add a pinch more salt to remaining gelatin and blend. Turn into pan over firm peach layer. Chill until firm. Remove from mold. Serve in slices onto crisp greens.

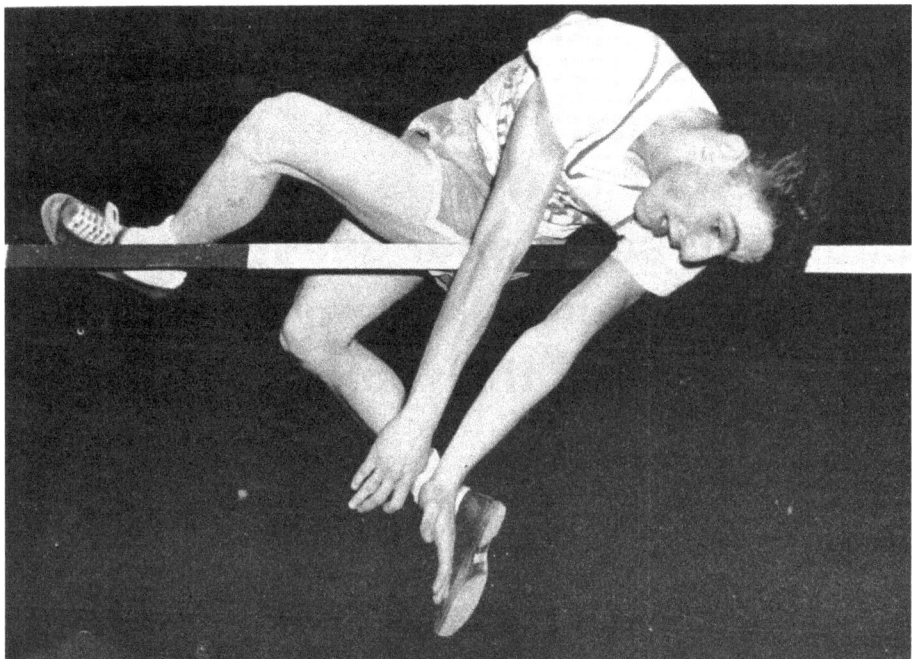

FRUIT

All types of fruit is always a good choice to serve your guest. Sliced or diced arranged on a platter or in a fruit bowl on the table.

FRUIT COCKTAIL

3 oranges

2 bananas

1 cup diced pineapple

2 tablespoons lemon juice

Remove sections from oranges, sliced bananas and combine fruits with pineapple. Sprinkle with lemon

juice and chill. Serve in chilled
cocktail glasses or small bowls
garnish, if desired, with mint leaves
or chopped cranberries

Grapefruit Crabmeat Cocktail

1 ½ cups grapefruit sections
1 lb crabmeat, cooked
1/3 cup mayonnaise
1 teaspoon vinegar
1 teaspoon lemon juice
1 teaspoon Tabasco sauce
 lettuce or watercress

Chill grapefruit sections.
Combine crabmeat with mayonnaise
vinegar, lemon juice and Tabasco
sauce. Arrange grapefruit sections

in lettuce or watercress lined cocktail glasses or small bowls. Arrange crabmeat in the centers. Top with a splash of mayonnaise.

Melon Ball Cocktail

1 cup watermelon balls
1 cup cantaloupe balls
1 cup honeydew melon balls
½ cup orange juice
2 tablespoons lemon juice
Mint (optional)

Chill the fruits thoroughly. Place in sherbet glasses or small bowls. Pour blended orange and lemon juices over fruit and garnish with mint.

Frosted Fruit

2 oranges   1 grapefruit
1 cup diced pineapple (fresh or
canned)
1 cup grapes
1 cup pineapple juice or ginger ale
½ pint lemon sherbet

   Removed sections from oranges
and grapefruit, add pineapple and
grapes. Chill fruits. Arrange in
chilled sherbet glasses or small
bowls. Pour ginger ale or pineapple
juice over fruits and top with a
scoop of sherbet.

Shrimp Cocktail

1 ½ cups cooked shrimp
 (fresh or canned)
 Lettuce or parsley
 Cocktail sauce (or other sauce)

Remove black veins from shrimp and chill thoroughly. Line cocktail glasses (or small bowls) with lettuce or parsley. Arrange shrimp on top. Serve with cocktail sauce (or other sauce to your liking)

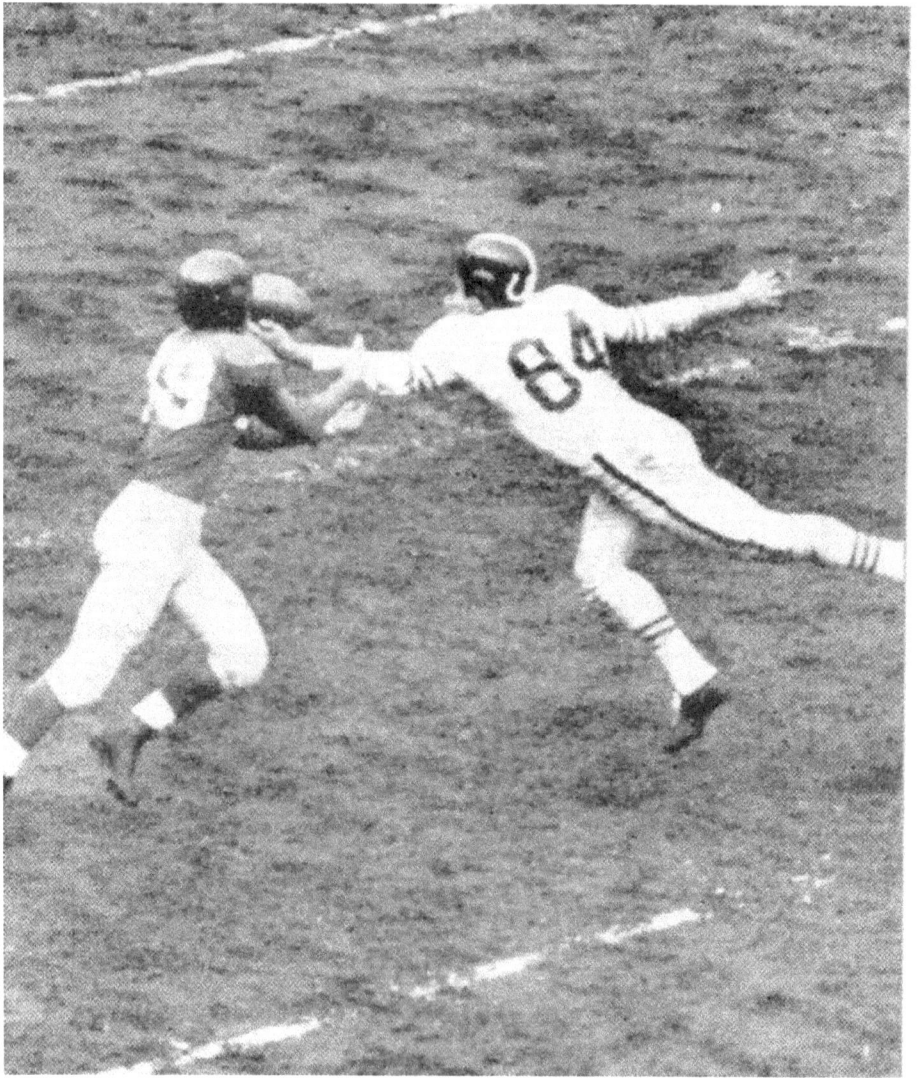

SALADS

French Garlic Salad Dressing

1 ½ tablespoons sugar

1 ½ tablespoon salt

1 teaspoon paprika

1/3 cup vinegar

dash pepper

2/3 cup olive oil

1 1/2 teaspoons dry mustard

1 teaspoon garlic powder

1 teaspoon onion powder

Combine ingredients in a covered jar, shake well and chill. Shake well before serving.

Homemade mayonnaise

1 ½ teaspoon salt

1 teaspoon sugar

¼ teaspoon paprika

½ teaspoon dry mustard

dash cayenne

2 egg yokes

2 tablespoons vinegar

1 cup olive oil

2 tablespoons lemon juice

Mix dry ingredients together. Beat egg yokes with a fork and blend with dry ingredients, then stir vinegar into egg mixture. While beating with electric mixer, add 1/4 cup olive oil very slowly. Add olive oil in increasing amounts.

Alternating last 1/4 cup with lemon juice. To make more creamy fold in ½ cup whipping cream.

Potato Salad

2 - cups freshly boiled potatoes (slice each potato in three parts before boiling, they will cook quickly)
1 - teaspoon salt
½ - teaspoon black pepper
½ - teaspoon onion powder
1 - tablespoon fine parsley
4 - tablespoon olive oil
2 - tablespoon apple cider vinegar

Cut potatoes in small cubes.

Add seasoning then olive oil (only the amount the potatoes will absorb). Then add vinegar and mix carefully until everything is absorbed. Place lettuce cups on platter. Scoop potato salad onto these. Sliced eggs and tomatoes make an attractive garnish around platter and serve.

Cheese and Pecan Salad

1 - cup cheese
1 - tsp melted butter
½ cup cream cheese
½ cup chopped pecans
½ cup chopped pimento
½ cup chopped olives
1 - teaspoon salt

1 - teaspoon cayenne

Mash the cheese with a fork, moisten with cream cheese and melted butter. season with salt and cayenne, add chopped pecans, pimento and olives. press into a mold. Let stand for one hour. Cut into slices and serve on lettuce with mayonnaise dressing or shape into small balls and serve on lettuce with French dressing.

COTTAGE CHEESE AND STRAWBERRY SALAD

2 cups cottage cheese
2 cups sliced strawberries
1/3 cup honey

73

1/3 cup olive oil

8 tablespoons lemon juice

½ teaspoon salt

3 tablespoons French dressing

Place lettuce and spinach leaves on platter. Blend together oil, lemon juice and salt. Pour onto platter with honey.   Mix cottage cheese, strawberries and French dressing. Arrange onto platter. Garnish with mayonnaise and whole strawberry's.

NUT SALAD

1 cup chopped apples (unpeeled)
2 tablespoons chopped
Maraschino cherries
½ cup chopped pecans
½ cup diced celery
½ cup mayonnaise or salad
dressing
Mix fruit, pecans, celery and
mayonnaise. Chill and serve on
crisp lettuce leaves.

Sport Salad

4 lettuce cups
1 medium-sized grapefruit
1 medium sized avocado
1 cup cottage cheese

¼ cup chopped pecan halves

arrange lettuce cups on individual serving plates. Peel and section grapefruit. Peel avocado and cut into lengthwise slices ¼ inch thick. Arrange sections of grapefruit and avocado slices alternately on lettuce cups. Place ¼ cup of cottage cheese in center of each salad. Arrange a pecan half on each section of fruit. Sprinkle chopped pecans generously over cottage cheese.

Carrot - Raisin - Nut Salad

½ cup seedless raisins
1 ½ cup finely chopped raw

carrots

½ cup finely chopped celery

½ cup chopped walnuts

¼ teaspoon salt

1/3 cup mayonnaise or salad dressing

¼ teaspoon lemon juice

Rinse raisins in hot water and combine with other ingredients. Chill and serve on crisp lettuce leaves.

Molded Fruit Nut Salad

1 package strawberry gelatin

2 cups boiling water

½ cup drained diced pineapple

½ cup orange sections

½ cup diced pears
½ cup chopped Brazilian nuts

Dissolve gelatin in boiling water. Chill until slightly jelled. Add fruit and nuts. Pour into individual molds and chill onto firm. Remove from molds and arrange on lettuce leaves. Serve with French dressing. Garnish with whole pecans.

American Quick Salad

1 small head of lettuce
8 thinly sliced radishes
small bunch spinach leaves
½ cup chopped parsley
¼ cup chopped green pepper
¼ diced celery

¼ cup chopped green onion
½ cup chopped ham
½ cup chopped bacon
 1 tablespoon vinegar
 salad dressing of your choice

Place a little garlic powder on bottom of salad bowl. Break lettuce and spinach in small pieces into the salad bowl. Mix in radishes, parsley, onion, celery and green pepper. Toss with desired salad dressing. Then add bacon and ham, toss a little more. Serve.

Simple Salad

2 cups chopped spinach
2 Cups shredded red cabbage
½ cup cottage cheese
 little salt
Lettuce cups
French dressing

Lightly toss together spinach, cabbage and cottage cheese. Season with salt to taste. Serve in Lettuce cups with French dressing.

Crabmeat Apple Salad

1 ½ cups crabmeat
¾ cups diced celery

1 ½ cups diced tart apples

3 tablespoons olive oil

1 teaspoon salt

3 teaspoons lemon juice

3 hard-boiled eggs

¼ cup mayonnaise

Lettuce.

Combine crab meat, celery and diced apples. Mix together olive oil, salt and lemon juice and add to the crab meat mixture. Chill 20 minutes then add chopped eggs and mayonnaise. Serve on lettuce.

Frozen Desert Fruit Salad

1½ cups creamed cottage cheese
¾ cup heavy cream
¼ cup chopped nuts
¾ cup chopped dates
¾ cup shredded pineapple
1 teaspoon salt
¼ cup salad dressing
Lettuce

Mash cottage cheese with a fork until smooth. Whip cream, fold in the cheese add nuts, dates, pineapple, salt and salad dressing. Freeze until firm. Remove and cut into squares place on lettuce and serve.

A FINAL THOUGHT

The people of the east have their
Kings and Rulers. The states of our
land are without them. Here we
have what is called a government,
for the people. To do what Is right.

Who accepts introduction to all people. Setting a high value on speeches of worth.
Being correct in conduct. Having no difficulty in overseeing the people. To govern and lead uprightly.. Government is supposed to be the greatest thing to man, For those who are near and far. Perhaps the government cannot keep its affairs before mind without weariness but to attend to them with undeviating consistency.

Not being an oppressive government (this is more terrible than your most dangerous criminal) to uphold right principles, so that there will be no distrust from the people.

When a country is well governed, poverty amongst the people is a thing government is ashamed of. To be willing to give and do what is necessary and just for the well being of the people.

Let us not lose hope in our country and our government, but let us allow our dreams to become reality and to flourish amidst the outer limits of mankind.

www.ingramcontent.com/pod-product-compliance
Lightning Source LLC
Chambersburg PA
CBHW061745020426
42331CB00006B/1360